GOAL!
LATIN STARS OF
SOCCER

Soccer Star
Cristiano
Ronaldo

Speeding Star
Keep Boys Reading!

John Albert Torres

Library of Congress Cataloging-in-Publication Data

Torres, John Albert.
    Soccer star Cristiano Ronaldo / John Albert Torres.
        pages cm — (Goal! Latin stars of soccer)
    Includes bibliographical references and index.
    Summary: "International soccer star Cristiano Ronaldo has already played for two of the sport's
biggest teams, Manchester United and Real Madrid. This sports biography will examine everything
from Ronaldo's childhood and early difficulties to becoming one of the best soccer players in the
world!"—Provided by publisher.
    ISBN 978-1-62285-222-2
    1. Ronaldo, Cristiano, 1985- —Juvenile literature. 2. Soccer players—Portugal—Biography—
Juvenile literature. I. Title.
    GV942.7.R626T67 2014
    796.334092—dc23
    [B]
                     2013014208

Future Editions:
Paperback ISBN: 978-1-62285-114-0   EPUB ISBN: 978-1-62285-116-4
Single-User PDF ISBN: 978-1-62285-117-1   Multi-User PDF ISBN: 978-1-62285-166-9

Printed in the United States of America
112013 Bang Printing, Brainerd, Minn.
10 9 8 7 6 5 4 3

To Our Readers: We have done our best to make sure all Internet addresses in this book were active
and appropriate when we went to press. However, the author and the Publisher have no control over,
and assume no liability for, the material available on those Internet sites or on other Web sites they may
link to. Any comments or suggestions can be sent by e-mail to comments@speedingstar.com or to the
address below.

Speeding Star
Box 398, 40 Industrial Road
Berkeley Heights, NJ 07922
USA
www.speedingstar.com

 Enslow Publishers, Inc., is committed to printing our books on recycled paper. The paper in every
book contains 10% to 30% post-consumer waste (PCW). The cover board on the outside of each book
contains 100% PCW. Our goal is to do our part to help young people and the environment too!

Illustration Credits: ©AP Images/Alastair Grant, p. 27; ©AP Images/Alberto Saiz, p. 40; ©AP Images/Alvaro Barrientos, p. 23; ©AP Images/Andres Kudacki, pp. 8, 13, 17; ©AP Images/Daniel Ochoa de Olza, p. 14; ©AP Images/Gero Breloer, p. 11; ©AP Images/Gregory Bull, p. 36; ©AP Images/Jon Super, pp. 24, 32, 43; ©AP Images/Luca Bruno, p. 19; ©AP Images/Narci Cuervo, p. 35; ©AP Images/Nick Ut, p. 25; ©AP Images/Paul Thomas, p. 31; ©AP Images/Paulo Duarte, pp. 4, 20, 28; ©AP Images/Scott Heppell, p. 7; ©AP Images/Thibault Camus, p. 33.

Cover Illustration: ©AP Images/Clint Hughes

CONTENTS

In his first season with Manchester United, Cristiano became feared by his opponents because of his aggressive style of play.

The Goal

It was a shot that not many—if any—soccer players would ever really take.

Cristiano Ronaldo, the star winger for famed English soccer club Manchester United, took a pass from one of his midfielders just past the midfield line. It was April 15, 2009. He dribbled slowly forward as defenders from FC Porto began backing up to take defensive positions.

A few days earlier, Ronaldo had recorded his first Champions League goal during a 2–0 victory over FC Internazionale Milano that put Manchester into the quarterfinals against FC Porto.

It was only six minutes into the Wednesday night match and both teams were playing a bit nervously. They were like two great boxers feeling each other out in the first few rounds of a fight. The play was slow and unsteady. The players looked as though they were running in mud.

He could have set up an attack by sending the ball high into the air towards the box. He even may have been able to make a run down the sideline where he could cross the ball to a teammate. But Ronaldo did something different when he was still about 40 yards away from the goal.

He decided to shoot.

No one shoots from that distance. Not many players are strong enough to score from there. Plus, the opposing keeper can see the ball pretty easily from that far away and move into position to make a save.

But Ronaldo is different than your normal soccer star. Very lean, the 6-feet 1-inch tall native of Portugal is extremely powerful, not to mention confident. Not many people have the power of a cannon in their legs. But Ronaldo has proven over the years that he can score from almost anywhere on the soccer pitch. What's even more amazing is that he is as good shooting with his left foot as he is with his right.

He set the ball up perfectly before him, rolling forward slowly and settling it. The brash young star uncorked a screaming line drive of a kick. The ball whizzed, slicing the air and traveling an incredible 65 miles per hour. The kick seemed to go faster as it approached the Porto net. It also started rising like a Justin Verlander fastball!

The keeper realized almost instantly that he was in trouble. He ran back, dove, and jumped into the air in what seemed like one fluid motion. But the ball, flying like a rocket, passed over his outstretched fingertips and exploded into the top corner of the net.

The fans long had a love-hate relationship with the star soccer player from a foreign country. But now they erupted in cheers and saluted Ronaldo with applause and waving flags. The ovation seemed to go on forever. It was a remarkable goal that players, fans, and sportswriters still talk about. More importantly, it was the only score of the game and allowed Manchester United to advance with a 1–0 victory.

After the match, Ronaldo was all smiles.

"It is the best (goal) I have ever scored," he told reporters. "It was a fantastic strike and I can't wait to see it again on my DVD. I am very happy with it."

Ronaldo has the reputation of being one of the hardest kickers in all of professional soccer.

While each player respects the other's abilities and skills, Ronaldo and Messi are strictly competitors when they are on the pitch.

The Goal

It was his 26th goal of the season and put Manchester United into the finals against FC Barcelona, which Manchester lost 2–0. The amazing goal would be long remembered by Manchester fans who soon learned that the goal would be his last playing for the team.

It is no wonder that Ronaldo—who was named after a U.S. president—is regarded as one of the two best players in the entire world, alongside rival Lionel Messi. They have clashed many times inside European soccer stadiums. Described by many as fast, elusive, and tricky, Ronaldo is also deadly accurate with his powerful kicks.

Soccer legends such as Pelé, David Beckham, and Diego Maradona have all said that Ronaldo is one of the best players they have ever seen.

But he has never liked constantly being compared to Messi because the two players have such different styles of play. He once told newspaper reporters that the comparisons made him tired and that it is impossible to compare two different types of sports cars because they have different engines.

But he does admit that when he and Messi are on the same pitch, they usually push each other to play even harder. Hard work is nothing new for the superstar known as "CR7" whose life has taken him from one of the most beautiful islands on the planet to the biggest soccer stage in the world.

It was hard work, after all, and the ability to overcome hardship, which has allowed him to make that journey.

Growing Up

On February 5, 1985, on a small island off the coast of the European country Portugal, Maria Dolores dos Santos Aveiro and her husband, José Dinis Aveiro, celebrated the birth of their fourth and youngest child.

The little boy was named Cristiano Ronaldo dos Santos Aveiro. The child's father had always wanted to name one of his children after his favorite American actor, Ronald Reagan, who later became the U.S. president.

Now he had done just that.

The Portuguese island of Madeira, off the west coast of the country, is known as one of the most popular tourist destinations in all of Europe. The land is dotted with lush flowers and beautiful beaches. It has famous wineries and the longest firework demonstrations in the entire world. It is actually closer to the continent of Africa than it is to mainland Europe. But it was Portuguese explorers who settled the island in the 1400s and claimed it as their own.

While the island is known for its wealthy and lavish lifestyle, not everyone who lives there is rich. In fact, Ronaldo grew up in a very poor part of the island. He lived in a small shack that had a tin roof on top. The tiny home did have one saving grace—it overlooked the ocean from way up in the hills of the working-class neighborhood of Santo António. The home was only about three miles away from all the lush hotels where the tourists stay, but it might as well have been a world away.

Even when Cristiano is surrounded by defenders, he still finds ways to score goals.

The family lived in the port city of Funchal, a very busy port for cruise ship liners packed with tourists. Ronaldo and his family could never afford to go aboard one of those ships that would set off for other exotic destinations. His father worked as a gardener but missed a lot of time because he had a very bad drinking problem. He would sometimes spend all the family's money on his addiction. This put a lot of pressure on Ronaldo's mother to provide food for the family. She was forced to work two jobs, mainly as a cook and housekeeper for the island's wealthy residents.

Even though his father had his faults and forced the family into some very hard times, he is the person who introduced his son to the sport known in Europe as "fútbol." In the United States, we know the game as soccer.

When he wasn't working as a gardener or doing landscaping work, Ronaldo's dad sometimes worked as the equipment manager for the neighborhood boy's club. Ronaldo watch the boys play soccer when he was very young. As soon as he was old enough to play, he was out there in his cleats and shin guards playing the game that is as popular in Europe as baseball is in the United States.

Even before that, when he was only two years old, his family members recall how he would play on the patio of the small home trying to kick a soccer ball.

Having watched the game played since he was young, Ronaldo picked up the sport very quickly. Even as a youngster he was very good. It helped that he basically

The amount of power that Cristiano puts into each kick has goaltenders worried each time they see him wind up to shoot.

spent every waking minute playing or thinking about soccer, even when he was supposed to be doing other important things.

"All he wanted to do as a boy was play football (soccer)," said his godfather, Fernao Sousa. "He loved the game so much he'd miss meals or escape out of his bedroom window with a ball when he was supposed to be doing his homework."

Ronaldo started elementary school when he was six years old, and one of his first teachers at Escola São João remembers him well. Maria dos Santos said that from the day Ronaldo walked through the school doors it was clear

Only the best players in the world, like Ronaldo, can "pick-pocket" their opponents. This is when a player steals the ball from between an opponent's legs while they are dribbling.

how much he loved soccer. She said he would sometimes make a soccer ball out of socks if there was no ball around to play with.

"He would always find a way of playing football in the playground," she said. "I don't know how he managed it."

When he turned eight years old in 1993, Ronaldo started officially playing for CF Andorinha, which was the name of the team at the boy's club where his father worked. He had been training and playing with the team before then, but could not be an official member until he was eight.

By the time he turned ten years old, Ronaldo was considered a "phenom." That is a term that describes a young player who is so much better than the kids his age that it is amazing—and that's exactly what he was: amazing.

And, with the proper effort and training, he would only get better.

chapter 3

An Emotional Player

Ronaldo has been known as a very emotional player ever since cameras caught him crying as he walked off the pitch, or the field, after losing the UEFA Euro 2004 Championship match. There was pain on Ronaldo's face as he wept and walked slowly to the locker room.

His father, José, defended his son's emotional display.

"He cried like the rest of us when Portugal lost the final of the European Championship," José said in an interview with *Inside United* magazine. "But he will play more games with the national team, and it was a good experience for him. He was angry to lose something that he shouldn't have lost. That's why he cried. It was the shock of it and the end of a dream. But he was still one of the best players on the pitch."

Whether his team is winning or losing, Cristiano puts all of his emotion into each and every match.

But his youth coaches know that Ronaldo has always let his emotions show when it comes to soccer. That's just the kind of player he is.

Rui Santos, president of the CF Andorinha team, said he remembered one game in particular when Ronaldo's emotions actually helped the team win. Ronaldo was barely nine years old and Andorinha was playing Camacha, the best team on the island, for the 1993–94 Regional Youth Championship.

Camacha was in the driver's seat with a 2–0 halftime lead. Ronaldo sobbed uncontrollably during the halftime rest period, and his teammates saw him. When he ran back onto the field after halftime, Ronaldo started playing better than he ever had before. He scored a goal, assisted on another, and led his team to a 3–2 victory that they still talk about on the small island where soccer means everything.

From that early age, Santos was impressed by Ronaldo.

"A footballer like Ronaldo does not surface every day," he says. "The first time I saw him, I knew he was out of the ordinary – he was more developed than the other players, different. But nobody ever thought he would achieve so much so soon."

News of a ten-year-old phenom spread through the island. The best two teams for older boys—CS Marítimo and CD Nacional—each wanted the young boy on their teams. The bigger, better, richer team, Marítimo, made a crucial mistake when they refused to meet with Santos,

Most players can walk off the field after a loss and be okay with it. But not Ronaldo. He is too passionate about the game.

who simply asked that the team that wound up with Ronaldo donate some equipment to his team.

Nacional gladly donated two sets of equipment to Andorinha, and Ronaldo was now theirs. Plus, Ronaldo always wanted to play for Nacional because his godfather, Sousa, had played for them years earlier.

Ronaldo made the most of his opportunity. He was immediately named captain of the U-12 team (for players younger than the age of twelve). He had a great season and scored many goals while leading Nacional to the team's first-ever championship. Many people who watched Ronaldo play that season said they believed he was already good enough to turn professional.

Try and imagine that. Try and picture an eleven-year-old boy playing major-league baseball or a pre-teen in the NBA. Yet, many were sure that Ronaldo was already good enough.

But as his play improved and his strikes became even more dazzling, his father's addiction became worse, and his health started suffering. He was on a downward spiral.

Despite his problems, Ronaldo's father José did not miss a single game that season.

A young Cristiano Ronaldo is shown right before his first match as part of the Portuguese national team. He was only eighteen years old.

"Those are most treasured memories," José would say during an interview. "Each time he played away, I had a place reserved for me on the bus or the plane."

He went on to describe the celebration that took place after the team won the title. He called it "unforgettable." José didn't know it at the time, but those games would be the last time he would get to see his son play soccer in person for a very long time.

Ronaldo would soon be going far away from home, but it would be the only way to continue his soccer journey.

After his one and only season playing for Nacional, the team was contacted by officials with Sporting CP, one of the premier teams in all of Portugal. Sporting was based in Lisbon, far away from the small, perfect island that Ronaldo had called home all his life. Nacional was not very eager to let the youngster go, but the club was suffering financially and Sporting offered to pay Nacional a lot of money for the rights to Ronaldo.

So, a deal was struck and the little boy set off for Lisbon. He would be away from his family, friends, and familiar surroundings for the first time in his life.

Ronaldo became homesick and basically focused all of his attention on soccer. He knew this was the lonely path he would have to travel if he wanted to make it as a professional soccer player.

Troubling Times

Ronaldo tried his best to keep his focus on just soccer, but it became more and more difficult. He was struggling at almost everything else. He had no friends, and the worst part was that Ronaldo felt different from all the other kids.

His accent and way of speaking was much different from the boys who had lived in Lisbon their entire lives. Some of the kids also looked down on the island of Madeira, where he was from, and made fun of it. He did not like being picked on and so he got into a lot of fights and arguments. He once got kicked out of school for throwing a chair because he said a teacher had insulted Madeira.

Not only are Ronaldo and Kaká extremely good friends, but they were also teammates and Ballon d'Or winners.

It was a shocking change for Ronaldo, who had always been known as a happy, smiling youth who had many friends. His grades began to falter, and his coaches at Sporting knew that he needed help. They contacted the boy's mother and convinced her to come and live with him in Lisbon to help him get better adjusted.

This was not an easy decision for his mother. She was leaving three other children behind and a husband who was not capable of taking very good care of them because of his condition.

She chose to go, and her son's troubles were soon behind him. This was very important in Ronaldo's development as a soccer player. Sporting, like many of the soccer powers in the world, has their own academy where

Ronaldo was only able to succeed in school because of his mother Dolores. After winning the English Premier League with Manchester United, Dolores (right) was there with Cristiano to celebrate.

Shown at a charity event, Cristiano is shown with some of the best players in the world holding each other's jerseys: Iker Casillas, David Beckham, and Landon Donovan.

young players are brought in and trained with the hopes that they will be good enough one day for the pro club, or even the national team.

The academy is known as Academia Sporting, and players train there in the soccer factory for many years. In Ronaldo's case, he studied soccer there for seven full years. Many well-known soccer stars playing for various clubs around the world have trained at the facility. Some of them include Hugo Viana and Luís Figo, who were Ronaldo's teammates during the Euro 2004 tournament.

But things were not easy for the future star. When he was only fifteen years old, doctors found a problem with Ronaldo's heart. It was called a "racing heart." If he were to keep playing, Ronaldo's mother would have to agree to let doctors perform an operation. She okayed the procedure, and Ronaldo was back in training in a few weeks.

When Sporting officials recognized that Ronaldo could become a great soccer player, they assigned private teachers and tutors to help him through his studies. They also assigned mental health experts, doctors, and counselors to help him adjust to everything from his changing body as he became a man, to his health, to being in a fairly new place, and the expectations that were being placed upon him.

But that was not all. The doctors analyzed just about everything they could on Ronaldo from his sight to his hearing to his bones. One special test they conducted checked the thickness of Ronaldo's bones to see how tall he was going to be. They believed that taller players should not play a lot of soccer at a young age, so they actually kept him out of games once in a while so his body could rest. The tests showed that he would be taller than six feet, and so they held to their beliefs.

In fact, even though he was the best player of his age group, it was six years before he was allowed to play a full ninety-minute match. He was seventeen years old.

The wait was well worth it. The match was against Moreirense FC. Ronaldo scored two goals to lead Sporting to a 3–0 victory. One of his goals was especially terrific as he dribbled around three defenders before smashing the ball into the net.

Being a very young player on one of the biggest club teams in the world might be a lot to handle for most people. But Ronaldo became one of the best right away.

He continued to earn more playing time, and started to amaze his coaches with his fast footwork, pinpoint passes, and dazzling goals.

But, oftentimes, to make it as a professional athlete, you have to be good and lucky. In a strange little twist of fate, just about the time Ronaldo began playing more games as a seventeen-year-old, English soccer powerhouse Manchester United signed a deal with Sporting to have them develop players for Manchester.

What really impressed the Manchester United players about Cristiano was his ability to be a dangerous threat on offense, as well as a hardnosed defender.

In another beneficial coincidence, one of Ronaldo's coaches, Carlos Queiroz, was also working for famous Manchester United manager Sir Alex Ferguson. Both were on hand to watch a "friendly," or an exhibition game, between Sporting and Manchester. Ronaldo has never said whether he knew how closely he was being watched, but it didn't matter. He did his thing and was simply amazing on the field scoring one of Sporting's goals during a 3–1 victory.

He not only amazed the fans, his teammates, and the coaches, but he also amazed players from Manchester United who asked Ferguson to sign the rising superstar. He was one step ahead and offered the young player millions of dollars to play for the English club.

This was very big news throughout all of Portugal and especially in Ronaldo's hometown where stories about him ran for weeks on the front pages of newspapers. Some said he was too young. Others wanted him to remain in Portugal and play for some of the bigger clubs. But everyone was proud of their homegrown superstar.

Within a few days, Manchester United had its newest star: Cristiano Ronaldo.

Manchester and Real Madrid

When Cristiano Ronaldo arrived at the headquarters of famed English soccer club Manchester United, the team's manager asked the young Portuguese player what number he would like to have.

Ronaldo, the first Portuguese player ever signed by Manchester United, thought for a while and responded with "28" since that was the number he wore for his club in Portugal. But the manager, Sir Alex Ferguson just smiled. He told Ronaldo that he should wear number seven.

Why is that important? Because Manchester only gives out the number seven to their best superstars. Ronaldo was given the number before he ever even played for them.

During his time with Manchester United, Ronaldo became known for making difficult shots, like this header between a defender and the goalkeeper.

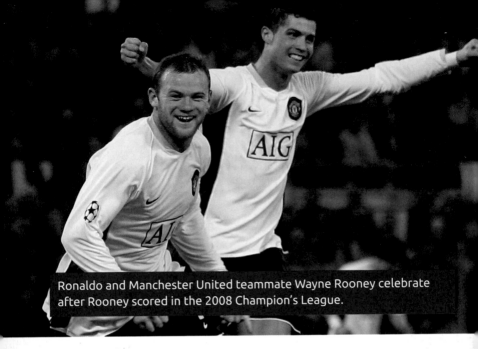
Ronaldo and Manchester United teammate Wayne Rooney celebrate after Rooney scored in the 2008 Champion's League.

Some of the players that had previously worn that number included legends like George Best and David Beckham.

Ronaldo called it an "honor," but also said he used the number to motivate himself even more.

There was already a lot of pressure and many expectations. Writers and experts were saying that, with the proper training at Manchester United, Ronaldo could become the best player in the world.

The young star scored his first Manchester goal on November 1, 2003 on a powerful free kick during a 3–0 victory against rival Portsmouth FC. Ferguson was careful not to rush the young player, who still had to grow stronger to compete with the grown men of the tough English and European leagues.

After winning the prized Ballon d'Or, Ronaldo kisses the trophy that he knows he worked extremely hard to win.

Over the next few seasons, Ronaldo continued to show flashes of greatness. He wound up scoring 10 goals during the 2005–06 season and fans gave him a special honor. They voted him the FIFPro Special Young Player of the Year. The best would be yet to come.

It was a special honor, but the Portuguese superstar was struggling with sadness that he kept to himself that season. His father, José Dinis, the man who taught him to play the game of soccer, died that year of alcohol-related illnesses at the age of fifty-two. Ronaldo missed his father very much, and it was at that time that he resolved never to drink alcohol or take drugs.

Despite his grieving, Ronaldo continued to reward the fans who voted for him. He was able to establish himself as a true scoring threat the following season when he scored 23 times. It was that season that other teams, especially Spanish powerhouse Real Madrid CF, started thinking of ways to sign the player away from Manchester.

The young player achieved one of his lifelong dreams the following season when he was able to represent his home country during the World Cup tournament that takes place every four years. He even scored a goal against Iran during one of the early games.

During a quarterfinal game against England, Ronaldo got into an argument with Manchester teammate Wayne Rooney, who was thrown out of the game for kicking a Portuguese player. The English media was very critical of Ronaldo and blamed him for the incident. The English

After his transfer to Real Madrid became official, Cristiano came out to a crowd of nearly eighty thousand fans to be officially introduced as a member of Real Madrid.

After scoring a goal, Ronaldo sucked his thumb and pointed to his son in the crowd as if to say, "That was for you!"

fans were upset with him as well, and Ronaldo responded by saying that he might want to go play for Real Madrid.

But he was welcomed back and continued scoring spectacular goals for Manchester in 2007, even though his personal life was in turmoil. Only two years after the death of his father, Ronaldo's mother became very sick with cancer. It was a tough struggle, and he tried his best not to let it affect his play on the field.

In fact, that season he played the best soccer of his life.

He led Manchester by scoring 42 goals, including 31 in English Premier League play. Because of that, he was given just about every award that soccer has to offer. He won the

Ballon d'Or which is given to the best player in Europe, the FIFA World Player of the Year, the FIFPro Player of the Year, the *World Soccer* Player of the Year, and the European Golden Shoe.

That special season was really when the world began to take notice of this great player and started comparing him to some of the all-time greats.

Spanish superstar Fernando Torres described Ronaldo as "massively impressive" and a "complete player" who was able to score from anywhere and with every part of his body. Except his hands, of course.

Other players said similar things. Yet, Ronaldo never quite felt at home with Manchester United and expressed a desire to play with one of Spain's top teams—Real Madrid. They offered Manchester more than $130 million to sign Ronaldo away, and so he started the 2009 season with a new team in a new city in a new country.

Maybe he was more comfortable because his native language of Portuguese is very similar to Spanish. Whatever the reason, Ronaldo was able to fit in right away with his new club. In an amazing scoring display, he scored 33 goals in only 35 games for them that season!

He topped that incredible season only two years later when he scored a whopping 60 times in 55 appearances —that's more than one goal per game. It also made him the first player in Spain's top league to score more than 40 goals twice.

He continues to dominate every soccer match that he plays with his incredible dribbling and impressive goals.

Just about everyone agrees that Cristiano Ronaldo is one of the greatest players of all time. But he has never received the affection from the fans or the sportswriters that some of the other players of his generation, like Lionel Messi, have received.

In an interview with CNN, Ronaldo said that maybe it has something to do with how serious he appears on the field of play. He always looks angry, rarely smiles, and sometimes gets into arguments with players from the other teams.

"I agree that I have a bad image on the pitch because I'm too serious," he said. "If you really know me, if you are my friend and I leave you inside my house and you share the day with me, you will know I hate to lose. I'm a competitive man and sometimes people interpret that in a different way, which is a pain on me because I don't like it, but I have to live."

Father, Video Game Star, and Philanthropist

R onaldo remains a very private person. In fact, even though he announced the birth of his son in 2010, Ronaldo asked his fans for privacy and has never announced who the baby's mother is.

But even though he is private, the millionaire superstar is a very caring person who loves to give back to those who are less fortunate. In fact, the player known around the world as CR7 was watching television one day in 2004 when something really affected him.

It was news of a terrible tidal wave, or tsunami, which had ravaged parts of Asia, especially the country of Indonesia. There, he saw a little boy wearing a number 7

Ronaldo is holding a sign that reads "Everyone is with Lorca" while he visited Lorca, Spain to show his support after the earthquake hit.

Ronaldo jersey. The boy had been stranded for more than two weeks all alone because his family had been killed by the wave. He survived by drinking water from puddles.

"This really got to me, after seeing the images I was really touched," the player told the Associated Press.

Soon after, Ronaldo visited Banda Aceh, Indonesia to help raise money for survivors' care and for reconstruction of the area. While he was there, Ronaldo was actually able to find the little boy, Martunis, who was about ten years old. He spent time playing video games with the child, helping his family personally with money, and, of course, playing soccer with him. He also gave the child several Manchester United soccer jerseys.

Ronaldo called the boy a "special child."

"When I met him in person and reflected on what he had gone through, it was rather difficult," Ronaldo told a television news reporter while there in Indonesia. "Over the time I spent in his company I noticed that he is quite a brave, beautiful, and healthy boy."

For Ronaldo's charitable efforts, that was only the tip of the iceberg. A few years later, he donated $100,000 of his own money to help build a cancer care center for the hospital that successfully treated his mother when she had cancer. It is located was on the island of Madeira where he grew up.

The following year, his childhood hometown was hit by a terrible flood. More than forty people were killed by the mudslides that followed several days of heavy rain.

There were many houses, schools, and other types of buildings destroyed. Once again, Portugal's most famous soccer player responded with help.

He arranged for a charity soccer match to take place that would include him being on one of the teams. All the money raised from the game went to help pay for the island's recovery.

He has also helped pay the medical bills of cancer patients, especially children. He has raised and donated money for other causes around the world that moved him.

In 2012, Ronaldo agreed to be one of eleven soccer stars in the world that joined "FIFA's 11 for Health Program." This effort aims to raise awareness to help kids live healthier, drug-free lifestyles.

In addition to helping others, Ronaldo has spent a lot of time off the field doing non-soccer-related stuff. Maybe it's because he grew up so poor. Whatever the reason, Ronaldo sure is involved in lots of businesses.

With the help of his two sisters, Ronaldo opened two fashion stores, or boutiques, named CR7—his nickname. Both shops are in Portugal and are doing well. In 2011, Ronaldo started a soccer game phone app called "Heads Up with Cristiano."

He also has been the cover and inspiration for several popular soccer video games including *FIFA Street 2,* as well as *Pro Evolution Soccer 2012* and *2013.*

As Ronaldo continues to break record after record for Real Madrid, there is little doubt that he is among the

With each passing year, Ronaldo continues to get better and better. If his career were to end today, he would still go down in history as one of the best footballers of all time.

top two or three soccer players in the world. He is often compared to Barcelona star Lionel Messi. Fans and writers unfairly criticize Ronaldo for not being as lovable as Messi, who is always smiling and having fun.

The comparisons to Messi are something that will always frustrate Ronaldo. But he really doesn't care about what the critics say. The only thing he cares about, and has ever cared about, is winning. He jokes that he even tries his best to win when he races against his girlfriend in a swimming pool.

He said that he will never change who he is on the field and that he will never be a phony and try to be someone he is not.

"I describe myself as a good friend of someone who is also my friend," he told CNN during an interview. "I hate to lose. I'm an honest and straightforward person."

True soccer fans and fans of the Spanish team Real Madrid don't need the smiles or personality changes. They just want—and need—Cristiano Ronaldo to keep playing soccer the way he always has and to be the kind of competitor he has always been: fierce.

Career Highlights and Awards

- UEFA Club Footballer of the Year: 2007–08
- UEFA Champions League Top Goalscorer: 2007–08, 2012–13
- Ballon d'Or: 2008
- FIFA World Player of the Year: 2008
- Onze d'Or: 2008
- *World Soccer* Player of the Year: 2008
- FIFA Puskás Award: 2009
- Pichichi Trophy: 2010–11
- Copa del Rey Top Goalscorer: 2010–11
- European Golden Shoe: 2007–08, 2010–11
- Trofeo Alfredo Di Stéfano Award: 2011–12
- UEFA Euro Top Scorer: 2012
- Football League Cup Champion (with Manchester United): 2005–06, 2008–09
- UEFA Champions League Champion (with Manchester United): 2007–08
- Premier League Champion (with Manchester United): 2006–07, 2007–08, 2008–09
- Copa del Rey Champion (with Real Madrid): 2010–11

- La Liga Champion (with Real Madrid): 2011–12
- Supercopa de España Champion (with Real Madrid): 2012
- Only player to win European Golden Shoe in two different leagues (English Premier League and Spanish La Liga).
- Scored his first official goal on October 3, 2002 as a member of Sporting Lisbon.
- Scored his 300th career goals on January 27, 2013 as a member of Real Madrid.
- Scored his 200th career club goal with Real Madrid on May 8, 2013.
- Fastest to 200 career goals with Real Madrid in Real Madrid's history (only 197 matches).
- Purchased by Real Madrid for the world largest transfer fee of €80 million.

INTERNET ADDRESSES

Cristiano Ronaldo Fan Site
   <http://www.ronaldo7.net/>

Official Real Madrid C.F. Web Site
   <http://www.realmadrid.com/cs/Satellite/en/Home.
   htm>

FIFA Official Site
   <http://www.fifa.com/>

INDEX